# PIECES

# OF

# ME

*MATTERS OF A POETS HEART*

*By: LaToya Williams*

*Trying to fill another's position is sometimes more difficult than you can imagine. You may not get very far trying to walk in someone else's shoes. But I can assure you that if you put on your own, you can walk a lot farther. And even into places that you would never expect. So, put on "your" shoes and walk with me!*

A Poets Heart

PIECES OF ME (Matters of a Poets Heart)
Copyright © 2011 by LaToya Williams
All rights reserved. No part of this book may be reproduced or transmitted in any form or by any means without written permission from the author.
Pieces of Me Publishing House © 2011

**Contact information:**
piecesofme33@yahoo.com

msharmonyus@yahoo.com

Facebook.com /LaToyaWilliams

419-322-0438

419-973-4961

Pieces of Me can also be found on Amazon.com

## DEDICATION

This book is dedicated to my mother, Rita Ann Williams. I love you with everything that means anything to me. You are to me a true example of a Queen and there is nothing or no one in this world that can replace you. Thank you for your smile.

Thanks for enduring circumstances beyond the comfort of peace, enjoyment and security. I know that you are blessed to prosper as you pursue a life of fulfillment, purpose and love beyond measure.

You always give me the reassurance of life, love and the freedom to be who I was created to be. I love you so much mom.

**YOU ARE MY INSPIRATION!!!!!!!!**

A Poets Heart

## TABLE OF CONTENTS

Foreword ............................................................... 6
Acknowledgments............................................... 7
Introduction ................................................... ..... 9
Sections............................................................... 10
The Heart Beats ................................................. 13
The Heart Heals ................................................. 29
The Heart Lives.................................................. 41
The Heart Loves................................................. 57
About The Author .............................................. 69
Heart of the Author ............................................ 71
Your Journal....................................................... 73

A Poets Heart

## FOREWORD

Life is full of obstacles but where there are obstacles we fervently believe they are plateaus for opportunities. Herein the author, poet, and dare we say, the oracle has penned MOMENTS in time that have shaped her life, framed her destiny and catapulted her into a place beyond the drudgery of pain and torment into a place of authority, depth, understanding and resolve. It's the resolve that defines the victory because the life and death matters are decided within the mind! For many, we interchange the mind with the heart in order to comprehend and correspond with one another. But as the poet refers to it here in this calligraphy of life, they are actually ONE in the same.

Go with this exemplary poet as she takes you on a journey that for some will never end, and for others will seem too short but for those who strive to be authentic and transparent they will find a resolution within the pages that will help shape, mold and characterize their vocation in this world, and if they can hear, in the next world as well. Take each word and let it marinate within the soul and refocus your life, frame your worlds, and take authority over what is yours!!!
Enjoy...

Pastor Richard Brown III

## ACKNOWLEDGEMENTS

First, thank you God for blessing me with the gift to use words in a creative way. You are the lover of my soul, my friend, and I am nothing without you.

Dad (Anthony Williams Sr.), you are never short of speaking a kind word over my life. I was considered your star even when I was in the womb. Thank you because words have power. I love you very much.

Denise, I couldn't have asked for a more loving and caring stepmom. Thank you for never treating me or my brother like step children but like your own children. I love you.

To my Siblings, Anthony, Alonzo, Dale, Tonisha, Teeousha and Taneesha knowing that you all are taking notes of my life enflames me with a drive to dream, pursue and achieve. I love you all more than you will ever know.

To my nieces, nephews and God-daughters Antyonna, Leah, Amari, Aleena, Alajah, Daion, Dailin, ShaKevia and Sabriah you all light up my life and every thought of you brighten up my day. "Hugs and Kisses" to each of you. I love you all so much.

To the rest of my family (way too many to name) and my dear friends, you all are precious to me.

A Poets Heart

To life, I don't regret you but I am grateful for you and the many changes that come with living. My experiences with you are priceless and I wouldn't trade them for anything.

Pastor Richard O. Brown III, I appreciate you for making it your business to provoke me to share my writings. And for inspiring me to write even the more. You are truly a treasure to me. You are also a true friend and pastor and I love you for that. Thank you so very much.

Last but not least I'd like to thank the woman who spent 13 years (and counting) of her life investing spiritual as well as natural jewels into my life. You have conditioned me for greatness. And I'll never forget the day that you prayed for the spirit of creativity to come alive in me. You mean so much to me. I love you Pastor Pat Mckinstry you are an amazing gift to me as well as the body of Christ. Thank you so much for your devoted life.

## INTRODUCTION

As we live this life that was passed on to us, we have many encounters. Although we have many encounters, we have been given only one heart to handle and deal with these instances. The thing about having only one heart is the fact that disappointments as well as happiness flows' to and from it. This sometimes causes conditions that are seemingly unbearable.

On the flip side of having one heart to get wounded means that there's only one heart that needs to be healed. Come and go with me as we journey through some of life's' most vulnerable but yet triumphant scenes or let's just say matters (of the heart). **TIME FOR TAKE OFF!**

A Poets Heart

**SECTIONS:**
        **(Intro)**
**The Heart Beats**
        Blessed
        The Beats that Made Me
        Purpose
        Art Is
        Pieces of Me

        **(Intro)**
**The Heart Heals**
        Yes Nonetheless
        Your Eyes Can't See Me
        Something New
        Will You Change?

        **(Intro)**
**The Heart Lives**
        Dance With Me
        Are You Going with Me?
        I Came to Give
        They're ready for You
        I Am
        I'm Free

        **(Intro)**
**The Heart Loves**
        He Loves Me
        I've Got Your Rib
        Without Chains
        I Love You
        Passion
        My Everything

## INTRODUCTION TO:

## "*THE HEART BEATS*"

I am always amazed to see how someone can be **pronounced dead** one minute. And in the very next minute you hear the doctor say these words; **"WE HAVE A PULSE."** What exactly does this mean? What is a pulse? What is the significance of having a pulse? Well let me tell you what it means to me. A pulse is just measly **BEAT** away from being **DEAD**. And yet in the same breath it is a mere fraction away from being **ALIVE**. **"WE HAVE A PULSE!"** means that what was once dead now, has the ability to **LIVE** again. **"WE HAVE A PULSE"** means that you have been given a new opportunity to pursue your dreams publicize your talents and even prepare the next generation for greatness.

Everything that happened before the **PULSE** is **DEAD**, **NULL**, and **VOID**. It doesn't matter! So, in other words the relationship or circumstance that would have killed you has just set you up for repair instead of reproach, restoration instead of reproof and recommendation instead of rebuke.

**Guess what people?.....**

*WE HAVE A PULSE!*

# THE

# HEART

# BEATS

**Your past is filled with precious rubies that can serve as life savers for others, so unlock the chest and disburse the jewels as you please, people are waiting;**

# *SHARE YOUR JOURNEY!*

A Poets Heart

## BLESSED
*(This happened when I was fourteen years old)*

Sitting in the front seat and dozed off one night
She didn't even hear when the car took flight
The enemy was lurking as he always is
Stealing is one of his goals and that's just what he did
He cunningly entered the car and didn't mum a word
This teenage girl was sound asleep until at once she heard
**LATOYA, WAKE UP!** God called her name,
She opened her eyes and noticed something had changed

The vehicle was moving and started going faster
This new driver was a stranger **what happened to her mother?**
She boldly looked him in the eyes and asked him **"Who are you? "**
This unknown man just smiled and grinned
She didn't know what to do
Still driving down the pitched black road
She questioned yet and still
Where do you think you're taking me?
His next grin gave her chills

He stretched his hand and raised the volume
But **SILENCE** filled the car
Although he'd driven her a ways
She wasn't very far

(Continued)

A Poets Heart

She looks and detects a familiar house
Her heart yet skipped a beat
Should she stay inside the car?
Or dive out into the street

The next three seconds of her life
determined what was best
She jumped out fell and scraped the ground
her clothes were now a mess
Cuts on her arms and legs as well
they felt like she'd been burned
The stranger was not pleased with this
he stopped the car and yearned

This young girl turned and realized
he wanted her no doubt
She yelled and screamed and called out names
**NOW** at her auntie's house
Persistently he charged at her
his fury filled the air
But when the porch light came alive
he ran and left her there

Hysterically she cried and cried
"please take me to my mom"
Not knowing that her frightened mother
was praying all along
Safely she made it back to her
now tightly in her arms
Mom looked and checked her baby girl
to see if she'd been harmed

(Continued)

A Poets Heart

The baffled officer said to them
"most girls don't escape this mess"
he smiled and told them they were lucky
Mom said:

**"OH NO! WE'RE BLESSED"**

## THE BEATS THAT MADE ME

**What I thought would kill me only made me stronger**

When those lights turned out and I couldn't see, feel or find my way
I felt the beats of my heart getting longer, timid and then the beats began to escape,
I moved around trying to touch the walls of my journey hoping that maybe the absence of gravity could influence the beats
And they would bounce off the walls and back into me,
As I reached and tried to grab pieces of me that so desperately oozed away, all I could feel was my present state conflicting with yesterday, wasn't until I stopped reaching that I was able to compromise with the lack of gravity and although I couldn't express it I felt a smile rising deep inside of me

**What I thought would kill me only made me stronger**

The memories in my soul started to fade they went from black to darkness and I had to close my eyes just so I could see the light, my feet started to move forward and the tighter I closed my eyes I realized that I was walking through the underground railroad there was hope in

(Continued)

A Poets Heart

knowing that the brightest stars shine at night
and though they are light years away they are yet
tangible, not because I can touch them but
because the essence of their purpose is fulfilled
through their shine

**What I thought would kill me only made me stronger**

When I gave you me and all you did was give
me history I could feel the beats of my heart
going from steady to an unsolved mystery
And although I wanted to I couldn't complain
realizing that today and history are one in the
same
So when I offered you me on yesterday I had
already given you today and a graze of
tomorrow
But I understand that because tomorrow may not
be fortunate enough to embrace my conscience
Today I take tomorrow and tomorrow I've
already taken yesterday
And the history that was supposed to stop my
beats had to release my wings and set me
free……..

**What I thought would kill me only made me stronger**

A Poets Heart

## PURPOSE

God designed me
He made me what I should be

I am the object to which one strives
I am the reason in which one exists

I am the target you reached on yesterday
The life that you live today and the goals that you seek for tomorrow

I am the wisdom you gain through your pain
The colorful rainbow after the rain

I am an intention an intended result the outcome of an invention

I am Adams rib that later became Eve
I am your blessing after you sneeze

I am your son your daughter your father and mother

The friend that treat you better than your natural brother

I am the rising and the setting of the sun
The reason from your calling you cannot run

I am the dream inside of you
That no one see's but God and you

(Continued)

A Poets Heart

I am the smile that chased the blues away
Because of me you will not lose your way

I am the matter at hand
The destiny of man

When others tell you that you can't
I am the force that says "yes you can"

I am purpose don't despise me
**I must be acknowledged; God designed me**

A Poets Heart

## ART IS………

**Art is** the feeling I felt when I first met you
And although you never touched me
Your strong presence drew me to you

Summons me with your electrifying style
The traces of your compassion pierced my
dimples and made me smile… huh…Art

**Art is** the look on my great, great grand fathers
face when he
Finally realized that freedom did ring
And that he could open and close his eyes when
and where ever he pleased

Didn't have to extol a "yes sir", "no ma'am" or
bow to the hand of the beast
But extracted the authority of his own hand
And yes! He passed it down to me

**Art is** the cure for sickle cell, the dead end of
cancer and the truth about aids
It is what compels me to turn my creativity into
productivity
And leave a lasting legacy to my great, great
grandchildren and their maids

**Art is** the message on Sunday morning that puts
a burning, yearning
Within the ramparts of my aspiration and
compels me to cling to learning with desperation

(Continued)

A Poets Heart

Seeking new ways to capture the monuments of life's uneducated education

**Art is** the acceptance of a culture that's not like yours
And the elimination of the societies that don't like yours
It is seeing the sun in a place without windows or doors
And escaping within your heart refusing to fight in staged, unfair wars

**Art is** the end of the great depression, the talented tenth that X felt was his best impression
The dancing around the ring before Ali completely pressed in

**Art is** the clothes that Oprah wore before they took her plus sized dress in
The millions that gathered before Obama was sworn in
My opinions of tomorrow when I pick up my pen

**Art is** the sum total of knowing you conquered granting the fact that you didn't even win
Art continues to go unrecognized even when it's at its best
But the essence of art is yet successful just as long as it is expressed

**Art is**............

## PIECES OF ME

**Here take my hands** and allow the tips of my fingers to tap away the stresses of your midnight
Receive the warmth of my palms as they relieve the tensions that are so heavily compressing against your shoulder blades

**Here take my eyes** and allow my sight to persuade your soul and observe the individual within, the one who hides behind the smoke screens of life
Let me see your unveiled desires deep into the contemplation of your intentions

**Here take my mind,** consume my thoughts with the beauty of imaginations, with the persistence of fairytales, you know the "happily ever after" where dreams don't just come true but they come through to those who refuse to die incomplete

**Here take my nose** as I inhale the scent of your value
Let me breathe in the qualities of your presence while the soothing aroma of your strength defines masculinity

**Here take my heart** and mend it with yours so that the vibrations of our beat can alert the heavens and inform the universe that the oneness of our arteries articulates endless possibilities

(Continued)

A Poets Heart

**Here take me**, hold me captive with the essence
of your honesty
Hold me captive with the power of your love
Influence me with your passions
Shelter me with the screams of your integrity
Console me with the silence of your security
As I give you **PIECES OF ME!**

## INTRODUCTION TO:

## "THE HEART HEALS"

After the beat is restored there are some things that need to take place in order for the heart to function at its normal capacity. We call this the **"HEALING PROCESS."** The healing process is very crucial to the life that can ultimately be lived. It determines if one will go back to living a vibrant, upbeat, normal life or a life of continual strain and stress in their heart.

During the healing process the heart must be handled with extreme care and delicacy. Rest and proper diet is absolutely necessary for the duration of this period. There are just some things that the heart need not come in contact with during this process if a full recovery is expected. Let's be careful as the **HEART HEALS…..**

A Poets Heart

# *BEAUTY FOR ASHES*

# THE

# HEART

# HEALS

**If you take the experiences that brought you pain or discomfort and use them as life lessons, then you have just turned what may be considered trash into *TREASURE!***

A Poets Heart

# *LESSONS LEARNED!*

## YES – NONE THE LESS

My heart says yes
My mind says no
Forcing my intellect
To debate with reality

My heart says yes
My will won't go
Trying to incarcerate my actions
Before I express them

My heart says yes
My hands are silently closed
Compelling my fingertips
To nudge against my palms

My heart says yes
But my arms won't reach
Embracing something new
Causes tensions between dimensions

My heart says yes
But my eyes can't see
Time is blinded by the suspicions
Of seeing in advance

My heart says yes
My legs won't move
Refusing to grove
To an unknown tune

(Continued)

A Poets Heart

> Yet and still
> I'm not compressed
> Because my heart says yes
> **None the less**

A Poets Heart

### YOUR EYES CAN'T SEE ME

**Your eyes can't see me**

All you see is what they see
Believe me if you could see me
The way I see me or the way he sees me
Your perception wouldn't be so shady

**Your eyes can't see me**

All you see is what they say
And what they say doesn't matter any way
Because I'm on my way
To a brand new place
I love this journey
Of each new day

**Your eyes can't see me**

Your vision is blurred
Not because of what you've seen
But because you chose to listen to what you heard

Allowed it to penetrate
**Why!**
**Didn't you hesitate?**
Take the time to evaluate, nope!
Instead you filled up your plate
Ate those lies like you were eating potatoes and steak

(Continued)

A Poets Heart

Washed it down with a tall glass of judgment
And self-righteously slept on it

Didn't think for a moment
**How true this could be?**
Hmmm Like I said

**Your eyes can't see me**

## WILL YOU CHANGE

Will you change for promise, promotion and the prosperity of your soul?

**Will you change?**

Will you change your environment for the possibility of greater substance, a greater portion, and an expansion of your right now?

Will you refuse to be compelled by what has been?
Will you refuse to be persuaded by the forces of your past and stop allowing them to restrain you and hold you hostage from the eruption of your future?

**Will you change?**

Will you erect your posture, level your chin and stride as one whose flag is still waving, heightened by the pole that stands on the same plantation that was supposed to defeat you and although they did cheat you, don't let the scandal confine you or hold you captive but know the power in your feet and continue to step, even if you have to ease on down the road don't be still, don't be stopped and don't be silent

**Will you change?**

(Continued)

A Poets Heart

Will you move from the dust of yesterday into the dawn of today and embrace the sunshine of tomorrow….

**Will you change?**

A Poets Heart

## SOMETHING NEW

The end of something old is the beginning of something new
Yes, the end may leave your bones aching and your soul cold without comfort

The beginning brings warmth that fills you and heals you and leaves you wanting more, refreshing you and making you, completing and intriguing you

The beginning comes with doors that one only imagines to touch.
Ahhh! How great it feels to actually open that door and walk through that door and shut that door behind you

Remembering what's behind the door not just as your life
But as a part of the puzzle that somehow fits and makes life what it is

Looking back and saying yesterday had some pain that was quite unbearable to bear alone and if I had to do it on my own I would have diminished trying to stand alone

But because I refuse to moan and groan over the ditch deep tombstone of my past I'm here smiling at you

(Continued)

A Poets Heart

Knowing that I'm alive not just because I live
but because I survived refusing to die

I put a tight lid on yesterday,
Not that it chased all the blues away

But I've learned that the end of something
Is whenever you say it

And the beginning of something is whatever you
make it
So do yourself a favor get violent with your new
and just **TAKE IT!**

### INTRODUCTION TO:

### "THE HEART LIVES"

See once the heart is healed and is in mint condition we can precede in **maximizing the use of our heart.** It is now that we can become more active and involved in everyday activity and exercises that would otherwise put pressure on a heart that is not healed. We can **now** begin to **trust and open** our heart with less restriction. It is **now** that we can offer our strength to another who may be in the condition that we've just recovered from. It is now that we begin to shape and frame our future endeavors to love, re-love and love again.

The steady pulse, nourishment of rest and rebirth has propelled us into to the state of not just **EXISTING** but **LIVING....**

**LIVE AGAIN!!!!!**

A Poets Heart

# THE

# HEART

# LIVES

**You're minding your own business and SUDDENLY your prayers are answered. Time waits for no one but arrives for everyone.**

A Poets Heart

# *IT'S TIME TO LIVE!*

## DANCE WITH ME
*(Inspired by "Decree")*

Dance with me
You have been summons
To dance with me

Collect your garments

Gather your flags
Raise the standard
Victory at Last!

**Dance with Me**

Wind up your twirls
Clap your hands
Stomp your feet
Spring forth and leap!

**Dance my daughter**

Submit to sound
Consecrate your movements
Acknowledge my crown

Embrace my throne
As worship is enhanced
Travail with triumph
**In Sacred Dance!**

## ARE YOU GOING WITH ME?
*(Inspired by the life and story of Richard O. Brown III)*

**Are you going with me?**

Because I'm on my way you see
Living in realms that was once just a dream
And when I thought that dream had died
That's when it was actually coming alive

He was birthing in me a new baby of advocacy
You do know they tried to silence me
Tried to put an entire generation on mute
This ain't TV

**This is real talk, real lyfe, and real experience**

Did I mention to you what happened the other day?
Yeah! They thought they could erase my face
Dismember me, replace my destiny with tragedy

Naw, that can't be because he hid me in the cleft of the rock
So when they did that 360 on me
It only brought me closer to the core of what's to be

Didn't know that I was like Daniel when I was in that den
They couldn't really touch me

*(Continued)*

A Poets Heart

So they locked me out
But it was only to lock me in

**Into what?**

I'm glad you asked
Into your future so that you don't keep repeating your past
Called me out so I could come in

**Come into what?**

I had that same thought in mind
Into my own time to be the leader of my own line
Huh! I'm the **"ACE"** for real this time

Oh yes! I wept and cried going through the process of time

**But it's a new day and I'm in a new place**

Done with the fuss and riff raff of old
This fresh season expands my horizons
Puts me above the snake line of the mountain

**I'm on my way you see**

**Are you going with me?**

## I AM
*(Dedicated to my lovely mother Rita)*

I am beauty
I am love
Not perfect, however pure as doves
I've been damaged
Yet priceless are my remains
I am stronger than the palm trees beating
Against the hurricane
I've been ostracized and criticized
But I refuse to be minimized
Though short in stature
I still stand tall
In soul in spirit in deed above all
I refuse to drain myself with worry, defeat or fear
I know where my victory lies
And that shelter is always near
I strive to be diligent in all
Grateful for all
And a guidance to all

I am wise
I know when my credit limit is spent
You won't find me walking around
Clothed in my rent

I am positive
Always thriving on the success of others
Never ceasing to console my sister
Or inspire my brother

(Continued)

A Poets Heart

My view goes beyond the outer shell
What I perceive I will not tell

I am the **glory of men**
I am the **strength of children**
I am the **masterpiece of God**

**I AM WOMAN**

A Poets Heart

### I CAME TO GIVE
*(To my "Rock" family)*

**I came to give**
I was sent here on assignment

To offer myself, my time, my talent
And yes my gifts

You see I do have a lot to offer
And priceless are the treasures that are within me

So here am I if I could I would
Give of every follicle of my being

**Applause! Applause! Applause!**

A great big applause
To you that is, yes to you, to you
And especially you

Truth of the matter is
I have received more than I can ever think to give

The treasures that you all possess are far beyond and supersedes so much more than one heart **(mine)** could possibly attain

Because you have allowed me to be the unique me

*(Continued)*

A Poets Heart

The me who was hidden in a cocoon
I didn't have wings yet
So flying was against the law

You have graced me to stretch myself and move about

**Thank you for opportunity**

Some say opportunity knocks, Nope! Not in this case

See from where I stand opportunity knocked the door down
Didn't wait for an answer, reply or a "come in"
You have given me more than I could ever imagine giving you

Because without opportunity, purpose has no real manifestation, no final destination

**I came to give** No! **I came to live**
To live in and to live out a portion of purpose

Fulfilling more than I could dream, so I challenge you to
Give your way into your destiny on purpose with each opportunity

Don't get caught doing nothing, but do yourself a favor and

**GIVE SOMETHING!**

## THEY'RE READY FOR YOU

They're ready for you
Where have you been?
Come from behind the scenes
And take them in

**Show them your beauty**
Unveil your scars
Give them a sample of what's behind the wall

Display your structure
And let them grasp
The substance of your journey
To help heal them from their past

They're ready for you
For the resources within
Your history can release them
From the shame that they're in

They're ready for you
**Are you willing to reign?**
To take them from
Dying to living
From pain to gain

The people are ready
Their hearts are open
If you take the stage now
They will no longer be broken

(Continued)

A Poets Heart

They're ready for you
**Are you ready my friend?**
To disclose your treasures
To let the nations in

They're ready for you
Give them your truth
Tell your own story
**From your point of view**

A Poets Heart

## **I'M FREE**

He was born for me

His blood he shed unselfishly

He was bruised and he was beat

Torment he suffered for me

He was crucified so freely

And then he died for me

But because he rose

I'm free

A Poets Heart

## INTRODUCTION TO:

## "THE HEART LOVES"

**Love is a wonderful thing** I once heard a quote that stated "it's better to have had love and lost it than to have never loved at all." I believe that almost everyone is searching for or at least expecting that special someone to come along that will bring an increase to their lives that only love can bring. I'm not just referring to naturally but also spiritually and emotionally as well. Love has a way of filling us up and makes us feel bigger and greater than we feel when we don't give or receive love.

I believe that **real love connects us to eternity** and it reaches far beyond the limitations of our natural bodies. It has a way of going deep inside of us, down to the pit of us, way in the innermost parts of us and it brings out the best in us.

A Poets Heart

# LOVE…
# LOVE…LOVE!!!

# THE

# HEART

# LOVES

You can't truly love the one you're with when your love is captured by someone else.

Love is never lost and yet it is always seeking to be found.

A Poets Heart

# *LOVE IS………*

A Poets Heart

## HE LOVES ME

**He loves me**

I mean the world to him
Not that I've never broken his heart or let him down

**Yet he truly loves me**

Not that I've done everything he always wanted, expected from or required of me
Still he really loves me

Though at times I chose my job, myself, desires, my friends, my foes, clothes and other materialistic, superficial, temporary, unimportant things over him

**Still he honestly loves me**

Not because he has to but because he wants to
Not because he needs me but because I need him

**Wow! He sincerely loves me**

You see it's not because I'm perfect, flawless and always right but he knows that without his love I can't sleep at night

He has chosen to love me not for what he can get out of or from me but for who I am.

(Continued)

A Poets Heart

**Oh, what a man!**

He has chosen to love me not because he can't live without me but because I can't live without him.

**Oh, how thoughtful!**

He has chosen to love and encourage me, promising to supply all my needs, protect, complete and comfort me, while making my dreams come true.

**He is God!**

And the same love that he has for me he has for

**YOU!**

A Poets Heart

## I LOVE YOU

I love you

Not because I have to but because I choose to

You make me feel so fluffy

The feathers of your sensuality make me blush

I am inspired to know you more than I know you

To give you more than you can reach for

It is me that I want to show you

The me you have not yet seen and even when you do see

You just may question, if it's really me

I Love You

Time cannot separate us
Space cannot evaluate us
Opportunity cannot fixate us
Death cannot emancipate us

I Love **YOU**

A Poets Heart

## I'VE GOT YOUR RIB

From the moment of the sunrise
To the opening of my eyes
As my vision penetrates through daylight

Your world is elated

Well, that's because **I've got your rib**

With every stretch of my limbs
As I continue to embrace this new day
Yeah, it puts an exhale in your soul

Your mind is refined
Just knowing that I rose this morning

You do know why don't you?
Because **I've got your rib**

You see, as I continue to move about,
Slide on my robe and take a stroll down the hall
into the restroom, you were watching

How do I know?

Cause I felt the sparkle of your smile on the
nape of my neck
And I heard your thoughts counting my
footsteps,
Not wanting to miss a beat.

(Continued)

A Poets Heart

And that's only because
**I've got your rib**

**Yes!** Your agenda revolves around my pulse
And your day is captivated

Knowing that every thump of my heart includes you
Hmmm… how exhilarating are the memories of
Me that rest upon the tablets of your intellect

**You need me, need I you**

We are intertwined

Soul to soul
Flesh to flesh
Spine to spine

**Why?**

**Because I've got your rib**

## WITHOUT CHAINS

Here I am
Loving without chains

Giving pass the pain of disappointments
And rejection

Using my life as a positive reflection
Has taught me true perfection

I knew you were the one
Even before I met you

Therefore staying in the regretful shackles of
my past
Is what I object to

So instead of living in fear
With nothing to gain

I Submit my heart to yours and
Love without chains

A Poets Heart

## PASSION

You enlighten me with your thought provoking ideas

The shadow of your integrity is soothing

And calms my racing pulse

Knowing that you have embraced my soul with yours

Gives me the security

To link my heart to your heart

And the only thing that is standing between us

Is the passion that connect us

**PASSION!**

## EVERYTHING I NEED

God I love you
You are so awesome

And you mean so much to me

Lord I thank you for your blessings
You have everything I need

In the time of trouble you hide me
In the night you calm my fears

I can never find anyone like you
You are everything I need

You are my rock
And my salvation

You are the song I sing
That leads me in your presence

You are my strength
You are my shield

You are my shelter from the storm
You are my everything

## CONCLUSION

As this journey lands, I hope it was as adventurous to you as it was to me. And remember:

*Trying to fill another's position is sometimes more difficult than you can imagine. You may not get very far trying to walk in someone else's shoes. But I can assure you that if you put on your own, you can walk a lot farther. And even into places that you would never expect. So, put on "your" shoes and walk with me!*

## ABOUT THE AUTHOR

**LATOYA WILLIAMS** is a native of Toledo Ohio and a graduate of The University of Toledo. She has been a teacher for the past six years. LaToya has a great passion for education and loves to teach and reach children. She is an active member of The "Rock" Church where she serves as a minister.

LaToya is CEO of "Pieces of Me" Publishing House and is looking forward to publishing, editing, writing and even ghost writing a plethora of books. Creativity flows through her veins. She is very much involved in the **"ARTS"**. Her artistic abilities such as singing, acting, drawing and most certainly writing are some of the tools she has used to take **"heart breaking situations"** and turn them into **"triumphant motivations"**.

The passion that she has to inspire others is astounding. Her refreshing poetic words erupted from years of journalizing. When asked why she is always keeping a journal. LaToya simply states "this is how I will be remembered when I die, because I will yet live within the written pages of my journey. It has been said that a pictures is worth a thousand words but a thousand words from the heart are worth so much more."

A Poets Heart

***THESE NEXT FEW PAGES ARE DIRECTLY FROM MY HEART,
TO YOURS:***

## THE HEART OF THE AUTHOR

I pray that the content within these pages have blessed, encouraged and inspired you. I thank you for your support and hope that you fulfill your earnest desires. If you know nothing else, know that you are a precious jewel and there is nothing in this world more important than the value of your life. You have made it up to NOW! Keep going and don't stop. There is a world that needs to know how far you've come.

This journey that I have shared with you is priceless. Some of the words are actually true stories that were compiled into poetic scenes. Some express desires that I long for as well as past hurts that I have conquered, while others are deep feelings that abide within the depths of me. Either way I have opened myself up for the world to see "**a piece of me**".

I must say that the journey was not easy and this new journey that I am venturing isn't a piece of cake either. I hold dear to the faith that "if God allows me to embrace a new day he will also give me the strength, bravery and perseverance to prevail over and through it.

Life is so full of surprises and sometimes we only know part of what the future holds. But I can attest that the part you know is enough to grab a hold of, push yourself into your destiny and pull yourself up to your dreams.

A Poets Heart

One thing that I have learned to do is release the pressures and cares of this world through my writings. I had to learn to write down my concerns or else I would carry them. I had to learn to write down my dreams and visions so that I could visualize them. I became accustomed to writing down the things that brought me shame, discouragement and pain, so that I could conquer them.

Writing is so essential to any healing method. So I urge you to **take these next few pages** and write. Write your dreams, goals, heartaches, heartbreaks, failures, successes, triumphs, disappointments and desires. Don't hold back anything. If you do, you will only be robbing yourself. So do yourself a favor, defeat your past, invest in your future and motivate an entire generation; by **WRITING!**

A Poets Heart

**FIRST YOU NEED TO OPEN YOUR HEART UP TO "YOUR OWN SELF"**
**(So many times we close our heart so tightly from the world that we don't realized that we've hid ourselves from our self) So take these next few pages and write a letter to yourself, about yourself!**

_____

_____

_____

_____

_____

_____

_____

_____

_____

_____

_____

A Poets Heart

A Poets Heart

A Poets Heart

## DREAMS

A Poets Heart

## GOALS

A Poets Heart

A Poets Heart

## HEARTACHES

_____

_____

_____

_____

_____

_____

_____

_____

_____

_____

_____

_____

_____

_____

A Poets Heart

## **HEARTBREAKS**

_____

_____

_____

_____

_____

_____

_____

_____

_____

_____

_____

_____

_____

_____

_____

A Poets Heart

## FAILURES

A Poets Heart

## **SUCCESSES**

A Poets Heart

A Poets Heart

## **TRIUMPHS**

A Poets Heart

## DISSAPPOINTMENTS

A Poets Heart

## **DESIRES**

A Poets Heart

A Poets Heart

A Poets Heart

A Poets Heart

A Poets Heart

**NOTICE!** I supplied more lines for your desires. We often spend more times on the bad things of the past instead of the awesome possibilities of the future.

**If you haven't already; get a journal and write daily. You will be amazed when you look back and reflect.**

A Poets Heart